NOVELLO HANDEL EDITION
General Editor: Watkins Shaw

THREE VESPER PSALMS, No. 2
Laudate, Pueri, Dominum (D MAJOR)

Psalm 113 (Vulgate 112) for soprano solo,
SSATB, oboes, strings & continuo (organ)

Edited by Watkins Shaw

vocal score (latin text)

Order No: NOV 070467

NOVELLO PUBLISHING LIMITED

PREFACE

Like Handel's settings of *Dixit Dominus* and *Nisi Dominus*, this work (not to be confused with his earlier setting of the same text in F major) was written during the months of his early manhood which he spent in Rome during 1707. It will be observed that afterwards he placed himself in debt to the opening chorus for part of his 'Utrecht' Jubilate, and to the concluding chorus for 'Glory to God' in *Joshua*. In No. 7 may be discerned a faint hint of 'Oh, had I Jubal's Lyre' in *Joshua*, and in No. 8 a pre-echo of some phrases in *Zadok the Priest*.

The present score is a companion to my editions of *Dixit Dominus* and *Nisi Dominus* published respectively in 1979 and 1985. Since my work on the latter, a detailed investigation of the provenance of source **B**, described below, has added powerful persuasion to what it was already reasonable to assume, and we may now regard as established that both *Nisi Dominus* and this setting of *Laudate, pueri, Dominum* (together with Handel's antiphons *Haec est Regina* and *Te decus virgineum* as well as his motetto *Saeviat tellus*) were composed for performance on 16 July 1707 (the Feast of Our Lady of Mount Carmel) in the church of S. Maria di Monte Santo, facing the Piazza del Popolo in Rome. Doubt must remain whether *Dixit Dominus*, composed almost three months earlier, was also performed on that occasion; but it is very far from impossible. In any event, all three are settings of Vesper psalms and all three were written in Rome in 1707. For further detail, see my paper 'Some original performing material for Handel's Latin church music', *Göttinger Händel-Beiträge*, Band II (1986), pp. 226-33, amplifying what I wrote in *The Musical Times*, vol. 126 (1985), pp. 392-3.

Sources

A British Library (Reference Division) [GB-Lbm(R)], RM 20.f.1, ff.1-29, in the composer's hand, dated Rome, 8 July 1707. In this score, with the exception of passages for Oboe solo in the first part of the last movement, Handel did not employ separate staves for oboes and violins, but used a common stave for Ob.1/Vln.1 and another for Ob.2/Vln.2, indicating use or withdrawal by directions such as 'Hautb/Oboe sol', 'Viol/Violin', or 'tutti' when both play together. This is generally serviceable, though he was sometimes forgetful and is not explicit about Oboe 2 in the first part of the final movement; also the duration of the notes on which the oboes end their phrases and some other refinements are

sometimes left to discretion.

B Pierpont Morgan Library, New York [NYpm], Koch Foundation Deposit 1085. This comprises 18 separate vocal and instrumental parts, evidently used at the performance in Rome, July 1707 (see my paper already referred to). Without doubt derived immediately from **A**, they are:

> Voice parts: (i) 'Canto Primo' (Soprano solo, complete, including the tutti Soprano I part of No.3, 'A solis ortu'), (ii) 'Soprano secondo Concertato' (the tutti Soprano part of No.1 with the solo phrase at bar 53, the Soprano II part of Nos 3 and 5, and the tutti Soprano part of No.8), (iii) 'Soprano Secondo Ripieno' (as ii, but the solo phrase in bar 53 of No.1 erased), (iv) 'Alto Primo Choro' (No.1 with solo phrase at bar 54, Nos 3, 5, 8), (v) 'Alto Secondo Choro' (as iv, but the solo phrase in bar 54 of No.1 erased), (vi) 'Tenore Primo Choro' (No.1 with solo phrase at bar 54, Nos, 3, 5, 8), (vii) 'Tenore di Ripieno Secondo Choro' (as vi, but the solo phrase in bar 54 of No.1 erased), (viii) 'Basso Primo Choro' (Nos 1, 3, 5, 8), (ix) 'Basso Secondo Choro' (as viii). Instrumental parts: (x) 'Concertino' (parts for Violins 1 and 2 for the use of leading players, with ample indications of voice or basso continuo parts, the whole expressed as a score of three staves), (xi) 'Ouboé Primo', (xii) 'Ouboé Secondo', (xiii) 'Violino Primo', (xiv) 'Violino Secondo', (xv) 'Alto Violetta' (Viola 1), (xvi) 'Tenore Violetta' (Viola 2), (xvii) 'Continuo Organo Primo Choro', (xviii) 'Continuo Organo Secondo Choro' (the word 'Violone' first written having been deleted by the scribe).

More than one scribe took part in copying. Some very slight attempt was made to correct the various slips or supply omissions in transcription, and it may be that Handel himself took a hand in this. All parts reflect his use in **A** in placing reliance on players' judgment where accidentals, though implicit by modulation, are not explicit in notation. The oboe parts are transposed down a tone, for high pitch instruments. No. xvii is figured, No. xviii is not.

String bass parts, whether for instruments of 8 ft. or 16 ft. pitch, seem not to have survived. But also comprised in Koch Foundation Deposit 1085 is a similar set of performing parts for Handel's antiphon *Te decus virgineum*. In this, three string bass parts are found: violoncello, violone, and contrabasso. In Italian terminology of the relevant period the term 'violone' was applied not only to an instrument of 16 ft. pitch but also to a smaller one of violoncello size. Presumably it is the latter which is meant here. As *Laudate, pueri* was first performed on the same occasion as this antiphon it is reasonable to assume it too would have had violoncello, violone, and contrabasso parts. If so, then perhaps the violone, a fretted instrument, would play in unison with the cello except where that is expressly designated as a solo instrument.

Perhaps it is not impossible that the alteration of the heading 'Violone' in the 2nd Organ part (No. xviii above) was after all a mistake. Not only is there no requirement for two organ parts of identical character, but whereas the 1st Organ part contains (with some errors) such figuring to the bass as Handel's score provided, the so-called 2nd Organ part does not. But if this was indeed intended for violone, it was careless to have included the bass part of No.6 ('Suscitans a terra inopem') without differentiation in view of the clear direction in **A** for two cellos and a double bass. Yet on the other hand, even accepting that a 2nd Organ part was not superfluous to the whole work, it was perverse to have included that movement, marked as it specifically is for 'primo Organo' by Handel. In the 1st Organ part of No. 4 ('Excelsus super omnes') bar 1 is marked 'Violoncell senza[?] cembalo ou org[a]no', the implication of which is elusive. The 2nd Organ part simply has 'Violoncelli'.

A comparison of No. i with Nos. ii and iii reveals that no copy survives for any ripieno singers of the Soprano I part of No. 3 ('A solis ortu') and No. 5 ('Quis sicut Dominus'). Certain of the parts distinguish in the titles between a 'primo' and a 'secondo' performing group. The texture of the work does not call for any such distinction, and apart from the brief solo phrases in the first movement, the respective copies are to all intents and purposes identical. This labelling must have arisen because *Nisi Dominus*, performed on that same occasion, does involve two such groups.

C Manchester Central Library [GB-Mp], MS 130 Hd4 v.205, pp.195-279, in score. Acquired by Sir Newman Flower in 1918, formerly in the so-called Aylesford Collection descending from Charles Jennens, and in the hand of S2 in J. P. Larsen's classification. Most likely dating from the 1730s and 1740s and almost certainly derived directly from **A**.

D Biblioteca del Conservatorio 'G. Verdi', Milan [I-Mc], MS 158-2. The first part of this volume (MS 158-1) contains Handel's antiphon *Haec est Regina* in the same hand. Its date is unknown, though probably mid-18th century, but its Italian origin and derivation from sources close to Handel's Italian sojourn are proclaimed by the ascription to 'Sig: Giorgio Federico Händel'. On the top L.H. corner of the title-page there is '177' within a half-circle, as if the MS has once been part of a numbered

collection. It has belonged to the Milan Conservatory since 1840, but only recent cataloguing has drawn attention to it (see Händel, *Haec est Regina virginum*, ed. Roberto Gorini, Breitkopf & Härtel, 1985; also R. Gorini, 'Un antifona di Händel "perduta" e "ritrovata"' *Nuova rivista musicale italiana*, vol. 19 (1985), pp. 62-73). In score, it allots separate staves to oboes and violins, but saves trouble by inserting musical 'ditto' signs for violins where they coincide with the oboes on the staves above.

I much doubt whether it was derived at first hand from **A** or any score directly descended from that. It may well have been compiled from separate parts or, at least, transcribed from an intermediate score so compiled. It contains features which, while not positively proving it, seem most readily explained on such a hypothesis. Thus, one doubts whether, in copying from a score such as **A**, a scribe would have bothered to allocate separate staves for violins and oboes, or introduced oboes in No. 3 and violas in the concluding tutti bars of No. 6, features not found in our sources **C**, **E**, **F**, and **G**, all in score. Furthermore, between bars 30 and 40 of No. 4 all the parts are jumbled out of range with each other in a way hardly possible to occur when copying, however carelessly, from a score, but not impossible when assembling a score from parts. If this hypothesis is right, the question arises whether it is our present source **B** that lies behind this score, with the oboe parts sensibly at untransposed pitch. Despite some minute differences of detail, its expression of Viola 2 in the alto C clef, and a little ambiguity about Oboe 2 in bars 11-13 of No. 4, it strongly suggests this by agreement with **B** in its most characteristic features, such as the anomalous treatment of the oboes beginning at bar 59 of No. 1, (see Textual Notes below), the large number of missing accidentals (additional to those omitted by Handel in **A**) in the Oboe solo part of No. 2, a common misunderstanding of **A** for Ob.2/Vln. 2 at the last quaver of bar 41 and for Vln.2 at the second quaver of bar 49, both in No. 4, and the introduction of violas at the end of No. 6. But this matter is of abstract interest only, without practical consequences for the establishment of our text.

E Royal College of Music, London [GB-Lcm], MS 248, in score. Formerly belonging successively to Domenico Dragonetti, Vincent Novello, and the Sacred Harmonic Society.

F GB-Lcm, MS 249, in score. From the Library of the Concert of Antient Music, existent 1776-1848.

G Bodleian Library, Oxford [GB-Ob], MS Mus. d.58, pp.163-235, in score. At one time owned by Philip Hayes (1738-97). I take the opportunity to observe here that this source, which also contains *Dixit Dominus* (pp.1-159), was unnoticed by me in 1978-9 when editing that work, though it does not modify my edition at all.

E, **F**, and **G** are of mid- or late-18th century date, in the hand of unidentified scribes. **C**, **E**, and **F** also include both *Dixit Dominus* and *Nisi Dominus*.

Critique of Sources

None of the secondary sources can be held to supersede the authority of Handel's autograph score, **A**, in respect of the essence of its text, nor do sources **C**, **E**, **F**, and **G** disclose anything relevant to our understanding of it. On the other hand **B** is important for its demonstration of how a contemporary copyist in close touch with the composer treated the instrumentation of such a score as **A** when drawing out the separate parts, and is therefore highly significant for certain details of the oboes and violas. At the same time, all the parts comprising this source reveal various slips in copying and a very large number of missing accidentals. Interesting as they are in illustrating conditions of performance in 1707 (to which a discussion, though out of place here, might well be devoted), they do not justify an exception to the general policy of the Novello Handel Edition of not furnishing a collation of secondary sources. Source **D** is in the same position generally as **B**, whether or not it is derived therefrom.

Accordingly, the copy-text for this edition is that of **A**, interpreted by **B** and **D** in what concerns the extraction of oboe and viola parts.

Editorial Procedure

Numbering of movements is editorial. C clefs for soprano, alto, and tenor voices are transcribed in the G clef, and the time signature **C** is rendered as $\frac{4}{4}$. Horizontal square brackets and quaver beams across bar-lines are editorial marks of re-grouping in triple time. Material in square brackets is editorial, likewise small-size notation (but not, of course, the string parts shown in No. 3), slurs marked with a dash (strictly limited to *simile* passages), grace notes, and short shakes indicated by ᴧ (a sign never used by Handel in music of this kind). I have marked consecutive octaves, not to show Handel up, but to protect myself against any idea that my text is mistaken. Handel's sketchy figuring of the basso continuo

is omitted as not indicating anything not disclosed by the obbligato parts. Cancelling accidentals required by the modern convention or to assist the reader have been silently supplied.

As to substantive accidentals and also ties, these are items which Handel recked little of, and were seldom adjusted by transcribers. To have noted every missing accidental and tie would have besprinkled these pages with special signs. For example, in the course of 11 crotchet values beginning with the third beat of bar 3 of No. 3, no fewer than 16 sharps are required in open score (14 in our slightly condensed form) of which Handel supplied only six. Yet at this point it is perfectly clear that his mind had settled in the key of D, as any student harmonizing this unfigured bass at the keyboard would be expected to perceive without the aid of accidentals. This was a habit of mind which persisted to the end of Handel's composing career.

To turn to an instance involving ties, can it be supposed, in view of the context of bars 50-51 of No. 1, that there is any doubt that ties are required at (a) and (b)?

One meets this matter of missing ties in heightened form in compound time – especially quadruple. At this period it had not fully escaped from being regarded as anomalous in notation, and particularly in 12-8 time Handel seemed as yet reluctant to write dotted minims and dotted semibreves (and, be it added, dotted minim rests). He preferred to use repeated dotted crotchets, which he frequently left untied when clearly intending to indicate sustained sounds.

In general I refer once again to my remarks on pp. iv-v of my edition of *Dixit Dominus*. It is not to the present purpose to put users into the position of picturing Handel's notation but simply to give, as carefully as possible, its meaning, distinguishing as editorial only actual departures from that. Nevertheless, where there may be even a scintilla of doubt I have denoted an editorial accidental by square brackets and an editorial tie by a dash, for example, No. 2, bars 23 and 41-2. One instance among many involving ties in compound time as found in No. 4 ('Excelsus super omnes') is discussed in the Textual Notes below by way of exemplification only.

Acknowledgments

I am most grateful to the authorities of the libraries which respectively hold the sources enumerated. In particular I acknowledge the kind permission of the Frederick R. Koch Foundation and the Pierpont Morgan Library to report on source **B**. Donald Burrows, Anthony Hicks, and Edwin Roxburgh have allowed me to consult them on specific points, while Sir David Willcocks was good enough to check certain details personally in the Pierpont Morgan Library. I wish also to pay tribute to Robin Langley for his helpfulness in numerous ways in connection with this production while he was on the staff of Messrs Novello. There have been frustrating problems, not of the making of either editor or publisher, and I owe much to the patient co-operation of Leslie Ellis, the Head of Origination.

WATKINS SHAW
June, 1987

TEXTUAL NOTES

These notes are confined (1) to matters relating to the copy-text **A** and the few departures of this edition therefrom; and (2) to details of our extraction of oboe parts in Nos 1, 3, 4, 8, and viola parts in No. 6.

Although information under (2) refers to the Full Score (F.S.) on hire in connection with this rather than to the present Vocal Score, it seems very desirable to make it accessible here. It should be understood that the details are adopted from **B** except where otherwise stated. In this matter the minute differences displayed in **D** are too trivial to record. The oboe parts in **B**, as explained above, are transposed down a tone. For purposes of these notes, citations from **B** are transposed back to the pitch of the score.

No. 1. 'Laudate, pueri'.
bar
2   Vla.1, 1st beat. The hastily written first quaver in **A** might be (and has been) mistaken for d^1, as also in bar 4, but e^1 seems required (cf. bars 74 and 76), consecutive 5ths notwithstanding.

Ob. 1 & 2, beats 3/4 in F.S.

7   Ob. 1 & 2, beats 3/4 in F.S.

13   Vla.2, 1st beat. Second quaver $\sharp f^1$ in **A**.
15-16   Ob.2. To avoid exceeding the compass of the early 17th-century oboe all notes after the first quaver are transposed an 8ve higher instead of remaining in unison with Vln.2

31   Ob. 1 & 2 in F.S.

41   Ob. 1 & 2 in F.S.

43   Notwithstanding Handel's 'tutti' at the last quaver of bar 43 in **A**, Ob. 1 & 2 in **B** do not enter until the beginning of bar 44. We adjust to conform to **A**.

45   Ob. 1 & 2 as in F.S.

Bass voice entry in **A** easily misread as d.
47   Tenor and bass voices, last quaver d^1 and d respectively in **A**.
59   Handel did not write 'tutti' here, though this is clearly a ritornello entry. **B** introduces Ob.2 (bars 59-75) but not Ob.1, which rests until re-entering at bar 74 – a curious anomaly, as the passage contains nothing unplayable on an oboe of 1707. We introduce both oboes here, doubling Vln. 1 & 2 until bar 75, which is treated (as in **B**) like bar 45.

No. 3. 'A solis ortu'.
Handel does not label the instrumental staves. **B** and **D** act on the assumption that the two highest staves are respectively for Vln.1 with Ob.1 and Vln.2 with Ob.2. We adopt this.
bar
16   Ob.2/Vln.2. When filling in the instrumentation in **A** Handel wrote the first two beats as thus differing from Soprano II. Whether by design or not, this avoids consecutive 5ths with Ob.1/Vln.1 which double the Alto an 8ve higher. But as Beckmesser would note, it now creates consecutive 5ths with the Tenor. We adjust to coincide with SII.

No. 4. 'Excelsus super omnes'.
Throughout this movement we employ a dotted semibreve or a dotted minim for Handel's series of dotted crotchets of uniform pitch, whether he troubles to tie these or not.
bar
1-4   Handel is slightly inconsistent in **A** as between *dotted crotchet* and *crotchet, quaver rest*. We standardise to the former.

11   Ob.1 & 2, 1st beat in F.S.

15   Ob.1 & 2. As bar 11 in F.S.
21   **B** and **D** ignore Handel's 'tutti' in **A** on the 1st beat, bringing in Ob.1 on the 2nd beat. (Similarly **C** marks 'tutti' against the 2nd beat.) We adhere to Handel's placing of the mark.
25-27   These bars may be taken as typifying the casual treatment of ties in such a passage. The rhythmic notation of A is

Source **C** adds ties after all but the 1st dotted crotchet. The vocal cue in the Concertino part of **B** adds ties after the 2nd, 3rd, 4th, and 6th dotted crotchet, but the Canto Primo part itself supplies none. Other different inconsistencies but of related character are to be found in bars 41 and 48.
42   Ob.1 & 2, 4th beat. **B** reads *dotted crotchet*. We adjust to *crotchet, quaver rest*.
48   Though this passage is exactly parallel to bar 41, Handel marks no 'tutti' on the final quaver. Consequently **B** and **D** do not introduce Ob.2, which we do editorially. On the 4th beat **A** has a blank in Ob.1, which should clearly be filled as in bar 41.

59 Ob.1, 3rd beat, treated as bar 11 in F.S. (though *dotted crotchet* for Ob.2 in **B**).

No. 5. 'Quis sicut Dominus'.
As in No. 3, Handel does not label his instrumental staves, but the use of oboes doubling violins is implied by his need to mark certain bars (below oboe compass anyway) for violins alone.

No. 6. 'Suscitans a terra inopem'.
In bars 90-98 Violas 1 & 2, not indicated beyond the direction 'tutti' in **A**, are introduced into F.S. thus, as found in **B**:

Doubling the basso continuo by otherwise unoccupied violas is a well-known baroque usage (compare Handel's explicit notation in No. 4). But it is interesting here to find the reinforcement carried an octave higher, even where viola compass would not otherwise be exceeded. It illustrates a love of a sonorous bass line.

No. 7. 'Qui habitare facit'.
There is no standard explanation of Handel's clearly written but curious ornament (or mark of articulation) in the violin part. Source **D** renders it as ∿. All other secondary sources, **B** included, transcribe it exactly. Perhaps it is best regarded as a heightened kind of staccato, or emphatic articulation (as by a particularly 'tight' rendering of ∿), even though the composer has already marked the violin part as staccato generally. Note that **B** applies the term staccato also to the basso continuo. But if that is accepted it can surely only apply to bars in which the voice is silent.

No. 8. 'Gloria patri'.
Throughout this movement Handel takes Ob.2 largely for granted, while making the Ob. solo part very clear in the triple time opening. We note below where in the Full Score we have followed the treatment of **B** and where we have differed therefrom.

bar
9-16   Ob.2 with Vln.2. (Oboe solo with Vln.1).
24   Basso continuo. **A** reads d^1, $\sharp c^1$, b. We adopt Chrysander's amendment.
33-42   Ob.2 with unison violins.
53-60   Treated as 'tutti' despite absence of any direction from the composer, i.e., Ob. solo, Ob.2, Vln. 1 & 2 all in unison.
63-7   No direction from the composer. Treated as Ob.2 tacet.
83-90   Ob.2 in unison with Ob. solo, Vln.1 & 2.
91-8   Though Handel marks no 'tutti' either at bar 91 or bar 96, Ob.1 & 2 are added to Vln.1 & 2, dropping out with crotchets on the first beat of bars 93 and 98.
100-108 Ob. 2 with violins, doubling Vln.1 when these divide. The first two beats of bar 103 are modified for Ob.2 as [music example] and it drops out after prolonging the first note of bar 108 as a crotchet.
113-14 Ob.2 doubles Vln.1, 2nd and 3rd beats of each bar. Unlike **B**, we treat bar 112 similarly.
115-17 Ob.2 with Vln.1, 4th beat, but regarding the 'tutti' as ending on the 3rd beat of bar 117, the first semiquaver sustained as a crotchet.
126-30 In **B**, Handel's 'tutti' in bar 126 is ignored, Ob.2 re-entering on the 3rd beat of bar 127 in unison with Vln.1. We have adjusted the re-entry to the 2nd beat of bar 127.

PSALMUS 112 (Editio Vulgata)
Psalm 113, Hebrew and English Psalters

No.1   Laudate, pueri, Dominum: laudate nomen Domini.

No.2   Sit nomen Domini benedictum, ex hoc nunc, et usque in saeculum.

No.3   A solis ortu usque ad occasum, laudabile nomen Domini.

No.4   Excelsus super omnes gentes Dominus, et super coelos gloria ejus.

No.5   Quis sicut Dominus Deus noster, qui in altis habitat, et humilia respicit in coelo et in terra?

No.6   Suscitans a terra inopem, et de stercore erigens pauperem: ut collocet eum cum principibus populi sui.

No.7   Qui habitare facit sterilem in domo, matrem filiorum laetantem.

No.8   Gloria Patri, gloria Filio, et Spiritui Sancto. Sicut erat in principio, et nunc et semper, et in saecula saeculorum. Amen.

DURATION ABOUT 20 MINUTES

INSTRUMENTATION

Oboes 1 & 2, Violins 1 & 2, Violas 1 & 2, Cello/Bass, Organ continuo.

Full Score and instrumental material,
including organ continuo part,
are available on hire.

LAUDATE, PUERI, DOMINUM

Edited by Watkins Shaw

G.F. HANDEL

1 Laudate, pueri
*Soprano solo and Chorus**

*With brief solo phrases for Soprano II, Alto, and Tenor.

20309

2

SOPRANO CONCERTATO [solo]
[f]
Lau - da - - te,   lau - da -

Editorial short score for rehearsal

5

20309

6

8

20309

2 Sit nomen Domini benedictum

Soprano

sit no-men Do - mi-ni, sit be - ne - di - ctum, ex_ hoc_ nunc,

ex_ hoc_nunc et us - que in sae - - - -

cu - lum, in sae - cu - lum, in sae - -

nunc et us - que in_ sae - - cu - lum, ex hoc nunc

SOPRANO

us - que_ in_ sae - cu - lum,_ in sae - cu - lum.

Oboe

(Oboe)

14

3 A solis ortu
Chorus a 5

1) As in No. 5 of 'Dixit Dominus', in this movement the strings almost entirely double the voices.
Expressed in short score this is unduly complex. The rehearsal pianist will find it clearer to read from
the open vocal score or may use the simple continuo type of accompaniment here provided.

18

4 Excelsus super omnes gentes
Soprano

1) Bars 5,6. One current edition modifies Handel's text at these points, also in bars 54-55, but this is surely unnecessary.

om - nes, su - per om - nes gen - tes Do - mi - nus, et su - per coe - los glo - ria

e - jus, glo - ria e - jus, su - per coe - los glo - ria e - jus.

Tutti

[mf]

Oboe 1   Tutti   Oboe 1   Tutti

Oboe 2   Tutti   Oboe 2   Tutti

2)

Ex - cel

Oboe 1

Oboe 2

[P]

2) Bar 25. For notation here and in bars 41 and 48 see 'Textual Notes'.

5 Quis sicut Dominus Deus?
chorus a 5

1) Bar 4. At this point the vocal and instrumental bass with figuring in Händelgesellschaft, Vol. 38, does not accord with A.

6 Suscitans a terra inopem
Soprano

1) primo Organo solo con due Violoncelli e Contra Basso

1) Bar 1. 'Piano' in Händelgesellschaft, Vol. 38, is a misreading of 'primo' in A.

2) Bar 15. From this point Handel's unsystematic slurring is here regularised in conformity with bars 1-9.

20309

i, _____ ut col - lo-cet e - um cum prin - ci - bi-bus po -

pu - li su - i, ut col - lo - cet_ e - um cum_ prin -

ci - pi - bus_ po - pu-li_____ su - i.
Tutti
Vln. 1

Vln. 2
Tutti

7 Qui habitare facit
Soprano

1) Bar 1. The meaning of this ornament is uncertain. See 'Textual Notes'.

20309

8 Gloria Patri

Soprano solo and Chorus

34

20309

S.D.G. G.F.H. 1707
d. 8 Julii Roma